Assisting Maths
Discussion Book 5

Peter Clarke

William Collins' dream of knowledge for all began with the publication of his first book in 1819. A self-educated mill worker, he not only enriched millions of lives, but also founded a flourishing publishing house. Today, staying true to this spirit, Collins books are packed with inspiration, innovation and practical expertise. They place you at the centre of a world of possibility and give you exactly what you need to explore it.

Collins. Freedom to teach.

Published by Collins
An imprint of HarperCollins*Publishers*
77-85 Fulham Palace Road
Hammersmith
London
W6 8JB

Browse the complete Collins Education catalogue at
www.collinseducation.com

© HarperCollins*Publishers* Limited 2010

10 9 8 7 6 5 4 3 2 1

ISBN-978-0-00-7221226

Peter Clarke asserts his moral rights to be identified as the author of this work.

British Library Cataloguing in Publication Data

A Catalogue record for this publication is available from the British Library

Cover design by Laing&Carroll
Cover artwork by Jonatronix Ltd
Internal design by Steve Evans and Mark Walker Design
Illustrations by Steve Evans
Edited by Gaynor Spry
Proofread by Jan Fisher
Photo researched by Fran Vargo

Acknowledgements
The author wishes to thank Brian Molyneaux for his valuable contribution to this publication.

Images
Page 4 Dreamstime.com: top left, David Iushewitz; top right, Robert Paul Van Beets. Page 5 Dreamstime.com: bottom, Albert Lozano. Page 8 David Towersey. Page 14 Dreamstime.com: centre left, Mark Huls; centre right, Sinan Isakovic; bottom left, Hunk; bottom right, Yuri Tuchkov; iStockphoto: top left, MBPHOTO; top right, Alexandr Tovstenko. Page 15 Dreamstime.com: top right, Cristian Andrei Matei; centre, Iryna Klimashevska; bottom left, Zakidrus; bottom right, Bodo23; Fotolia.com: top left, Maksim Shmeljov; iStockphoto: bottom centre, Arpad Benedek. Page 18 Dreamstime.com: centre left, Jennifer Thompson; iStockphoto: top left, Linda Steward; centre right, Nicholas Belton; David Towersey: bottom right. Page 19 Dreamstime.com: top left, Alexei Dobrovolski; top right, Alain Juteau; bottom left, Ahmet Ihsan Ariturk; Fotolia.com: centre above, Robert Hackett. Page 23 Dreamstime.com: top right, Maksym Yemelyanov; centre left, Haywiremedia; bottom left, Thien Vui Fah; bottom right, Darrenw; Fotolia.com: centre right, Chris Harvey; iStockphoto: top left, Radu Razvan; centre above, Guy Erwood. Page 28 David Towersey: centre. Page 29 David Towersey: centre. Page 64-65 Map: © Collins Bartholomew 2009. Page 68 Dreamstime.com: top left, Jf Halbrooks; top right, Paul Hampton; bottom left, Vlad Ageshin; bottom centre, Mario Savoia; bottom right, Nikolai Sorokin. Page 69 Dreamstime.com: top left, Stanko07, top right, Sergey Kolesnikov; bottom left, Simon Krzic; Fotolia.com: bottom right, Karam Miri.

Printed and bound by Printing Express, Hong Kong

Contents

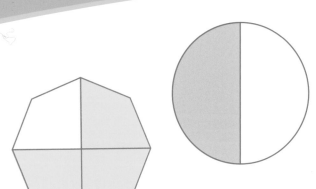

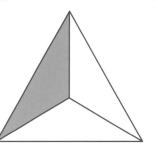

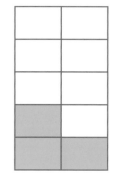

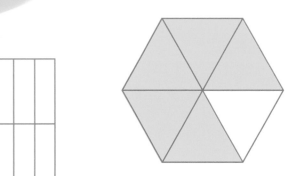

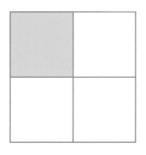

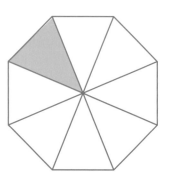

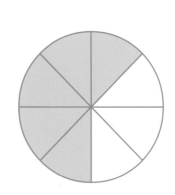

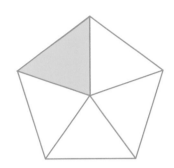

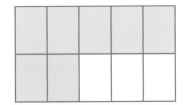

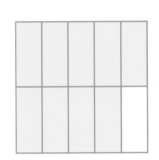

Save 1/3

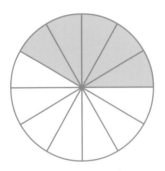

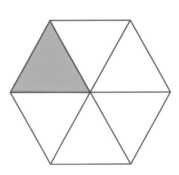

FOR THE CRUNCHY TOPPING
1ltr vegetable oil
3 soft tortillas, rolled up and thinly sliced into 0.5cm
(¼in) strips
1 red onion, peeled and thinly sliced about 0.5cm (¼in) thick

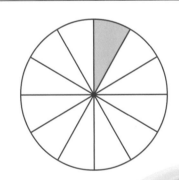

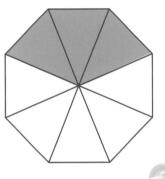

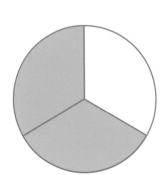

1									
$\frac{1}{2}$	$\frac{1}{3}$	$\frac{1}{4}$	$\frac{1}{5}$	$\frac{1}{6}$	$\frac{1}{8}$	$\frac{1}{9}$	$\frac{1}{10}$	$\frac{1}{12}$

×	1	2	3	4	5	6	7	8	9	10
1	1	2	3	4	5	6	7	8	9	10
2	2	4	6	8	10	12	14	16	18	20
3	3	6	9	12	15	18	21	24	27	30
4	4	8	12	16	20	24	28	32	36	40
5	5	10	15	20	25	30	35	40	45	50
6	6	12	18	24	30	36	42	48	54	60
7	7	14	21	28	35	42	49	56	63	70
8	8	16	24	32	40	48	56	64	72	80
9	9	18	27	36	45	54	63	72	81	90
10	10	20	30	40	50	60	70	80	90	100

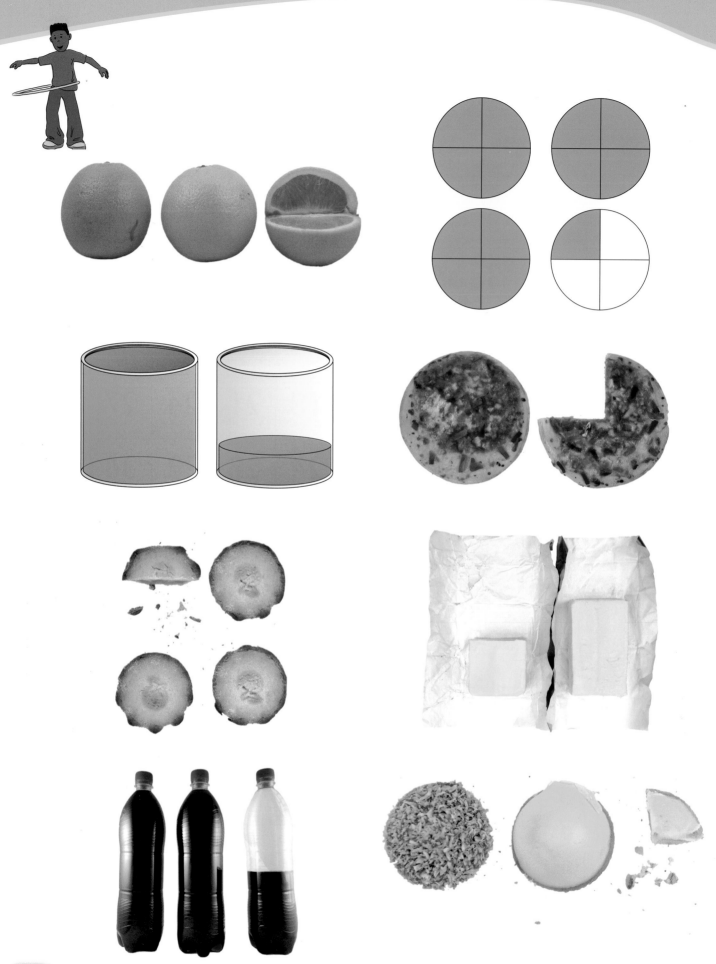

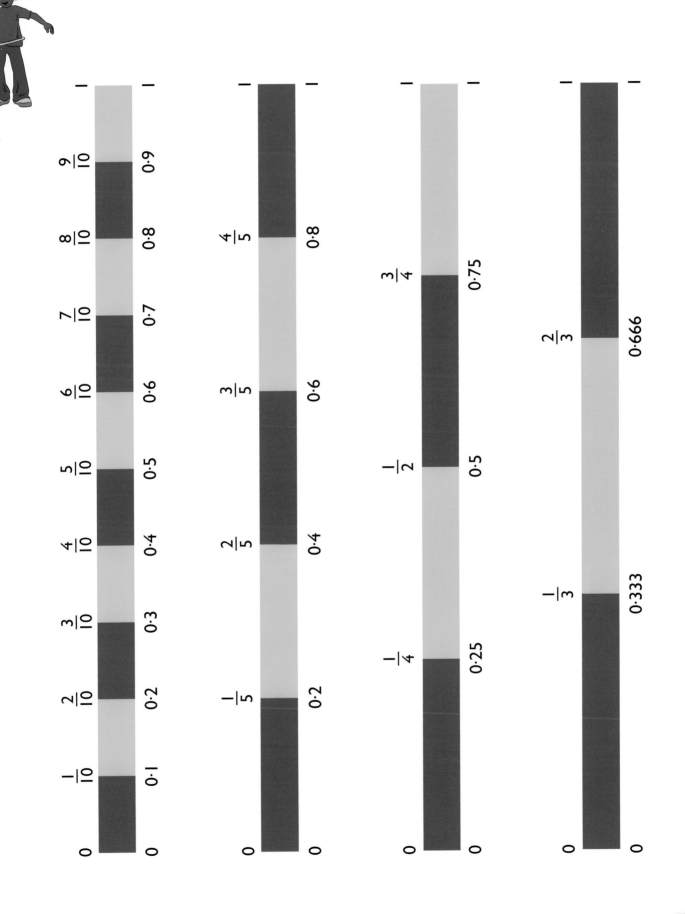

$\dfrac{2}{3}$

$\dfrac{1}{2}$

$\dfrac{4}{10}$

$\dfrac{1}{10}$

$\dfrac{6}{10}$

$\dfrac{7}{10}$

$\dfrac{3}{4}$

$\dfrac{3}{10}$

$\dfrac{5}{10}$

$\dfrac{2}{10}$

$\dfrac{1}{4}$

$\dfrac{8}{10}$

$\dfrac{2}{5}$

$\dfrac{3}{5}$

$\dfrac{1}{5}$

$\dfrac{4}{5}$

$\dfrac{1}{3}$

$\dfrac{9}{10}$

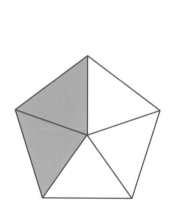

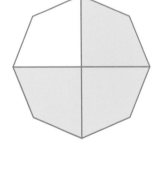

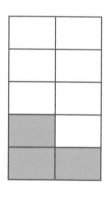

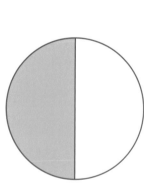

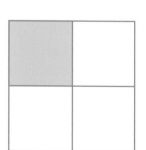

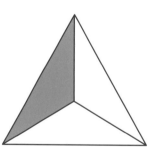

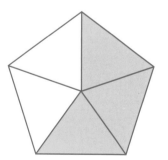

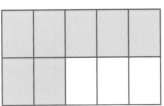

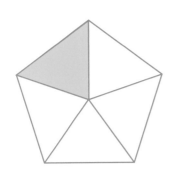

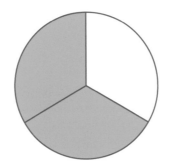

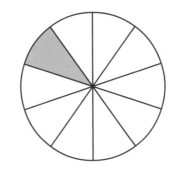

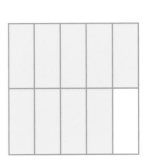

0·25

0·333

0·6

0·1

0·5

0·2

0·7

0·9

0·666

0·75

0·3

0·4

0·8

9 000 000	900 000	90 000	9000	900	90	9
8 000 000	800 000	80 000	8000	800	80	8
7 000 000	700 000	70 000	7000	700	70	7
6 000 000	600 000	60 000	6000	600	60	6
5 000 000	500 000	50 000	5000	500	50	5
4 000 000	400 000	40 000	4000	400	40	4
3 000 000	300 000	30 000	3000	300	30	3
2 000 000	200 000	20 000	2000	200	20	2
1 000 000	100 000	10 000	1000	100	10	1

1000	100	10	1	0·1	0·01
2000	200	20	2	0·2	0·02
3000	300	30	3	0·3	0·03
4000	400	40	4	0·4	0·04
5000	500	50	5	0·5	0·05
6000	600	60	6	0·6	0·06
7000	700	70	7	0·7	0·07
8000	800	80	8	0·8	0·08
9000	900	90	9	0·9	0·09

120 140 160 180
100 200
80 220
60 240
40 260
20 0 280
500 ml
400
300
200
100
dL 5
4,5
4
3,5
3
2,5
2
1,5
1
15 16 17 18 19 20 21 22 23 24 25 26 27
2000 g
1500
1000
80 100 120 140
60 160
40 180
20 200
220
km/h
W=1083
188036
488

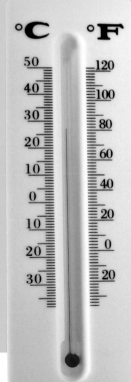

Decimal between

A game for 2 players

You need:
- two 1–6 dice
- counters in two different colours

Before you start:
- Decide which game to play.
- Choose who will have which coloured counters.

Take turns to:
- Roll both dice, e.g. 3 and 4 (if you roll a double, roll the dice again).
- Place one of your counters on the board on a decimal which is between the two dice numbers, e.g. 3·6.

The winner is the first player to make a line using 3 of their counters. A line can be along a row or a column or a diagonal.

Tenths game

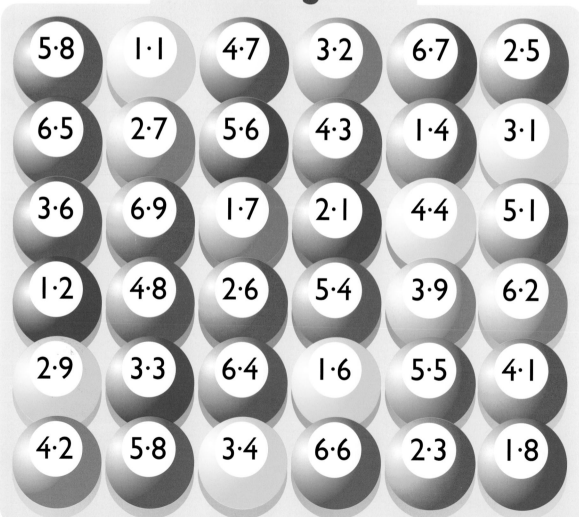

5·8	1·1	4·7	3·2	6·7	2·5
6·5	2·7	5·6	4·3	1·4	3·1
3·6	6·9	1·7	2·1	4·4	5·1
1·2	4·8	2·6	5·4	3·9	6·2
2·9	3·3	6·4	1·6	5·5	4·1
4·2	5·8	3·4	6·6	2·3	1·8

Tenths and hundredths game

3·5	6·71	2·36	5·32	1·5	4·3
1·23	4·4	3·64	2·1	6·8	5·56
5·65	1·6	6·07	4·7	2·78	3·8
6·1	2·52	4·01	3·93	5·9	1·4
4·24	5·2	1·3	6·55	3·17	2·2
2·28	3·4	5·5	1·89	4·56	6·9

SPROUT STEMS £ 1.30 EACH

SAVE £53.89

Wood Screws

Slotted countersunk Brass

- Suitable for indoor use
- Use with brass fittings

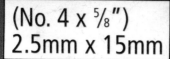

(No. 4 x ⅝") 2.5mm x 15mm	Qty. 25

Red kidney beans in water

Ingredients
Red kidney beans, Water, Firming agent (calcium chloride).

Produced in a factory which uses nut, peanut and sesame ingredients

3 heaped tablespoons of beans provides you with 1 of your recommended daily portions of fruit and vegetables

Nutrition Typical values	per 100g (drained)	per ½ can (drained)
Energy	385kJ/93kcal	462kJ/112kcal
Protein	7.1g	8.5g
Carbohydrates	14.8g	17.8g
of which sugars	0.9g	1.1g
Fat	0.6g	0.7g
of which saturates	0.1g	0.1g
Fibre	5.7g	6.8g
Sodium	trace	trace
Salt equivalent	trace	trace

	per ½ can (drained) %GDA	your GDA*
Energy	5.6%	2000kcal
Sugars	1.2%	90g
Fat	1%	70g
Saturates	0.5%	20g
Salt equivalent	trace	6g

*Recommended guideline daily amounts (GDA) average adult (women)

How to cook
Cooking appliances vary. These instructions are given as a guide.
Please ensure that the product is piping hot throughout before serving.
Hob - Empty contents into a saucepan. Heat gently for 3-4 minutes, stirring frequently. Do not allow to boil as this will impair flavour.
Microwave - Empty contents into a non-metallic bowl and cover. Cook on full power for 4 mins (Cat B/650W), 3½ mins (Cat D/750W) stirring halfway through cooking.

How to store
Store in a cool dry place. Once opened, transfer into a non-metallic container, keep refrigerated and consume within 48 hours.

410g

This can is 100% recyclable

To find out about recycling in your area visit www.recyclenow.com

Produced in the U
FOR BEST BEFORE DATE
SEE END OF CAN
Suitable for vegetarians

Customer Services Helpline
www.morrisons.co.uk
Wm Morrison Supermarkets
Gain Lane, Bradford, BD3 7DL

We're here to help

0.3
0.2 mm 0.4
0.1 0.5
0 0.6

2.4 m

7.5 T

1000000
% OFF ON/c
√ M- M+ CE
MR/c M- 9 ÷
7 8 9 ×
4 5 6 −
1 2 3 +
0 . =

ONLY
£4.99
for 360!

Buy any two £19.59 games for £30

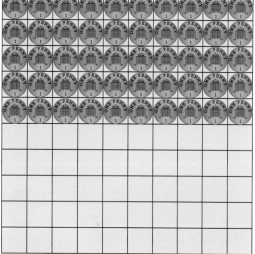

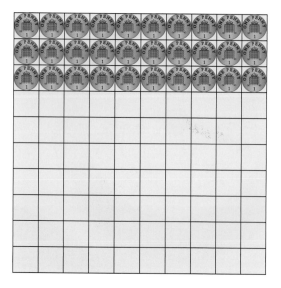

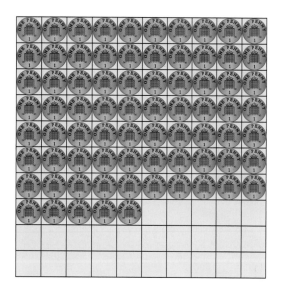

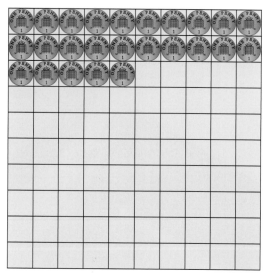

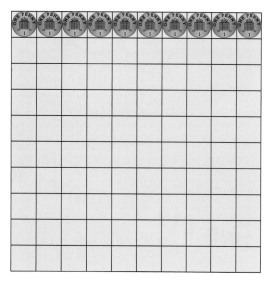

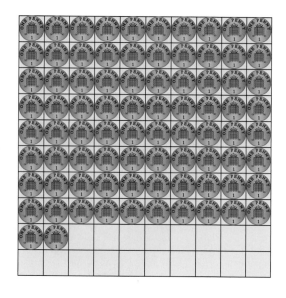

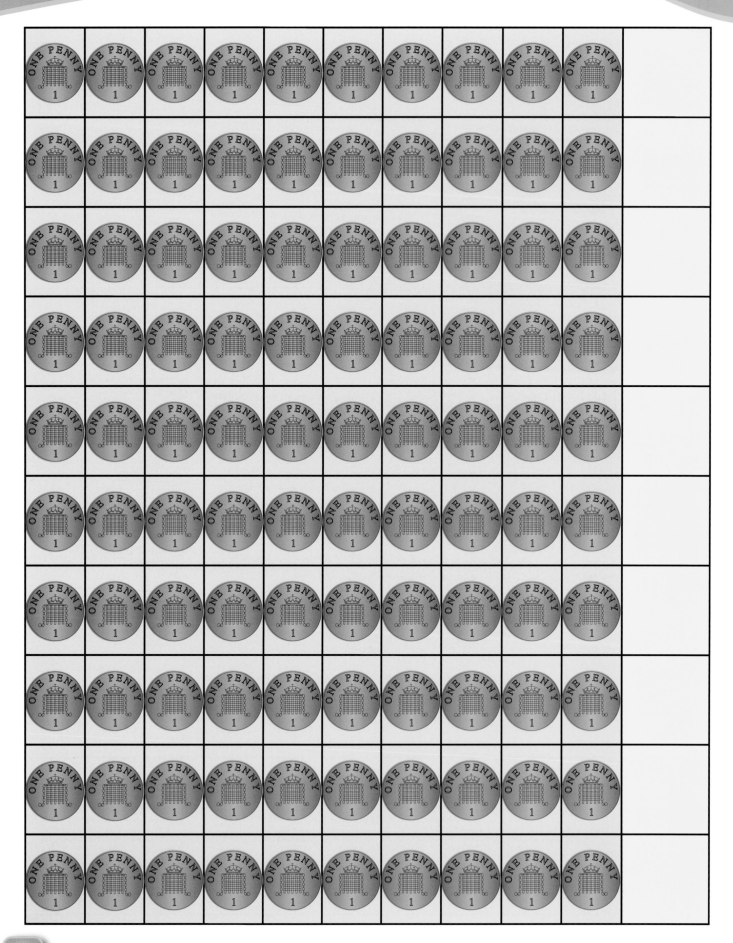

$\frac{1}{10}$

$\frac{1}{5}$

$\frac{6}{10}$

$\frac{2}{5}$

$\frac{7}{10}$

$\frac{3}{10}$

$\frac{4}{5}$

$\frac{4}{10}$

$\frac{3}{5}$

$\frac{8}{10}$

$\frac{1}{2}$

$\frac{5}{10}$

$\frac{9}{10}$

$\frac{2}{10}$

0·1

0·7

0·8

0·9

0·3

0·6

0·4

0·5

0·2

$\dfrac{1}{100}$

$\dfrac{68}{100}$

$\dfrac{5}{100}$

$\dfrac{99}{100}$

$\dfrac{1}{4}$

$\dfrac{25}{100}$

$\dfrac{75}{100}$

$\dfrac{74}{100}$

$\dfrac{2}{100}$

$\dfrac{46}{100}$

$\dfrac{3}{4}$

0·25

0·68

0·02

0·05

0·75

0·46

0·74

0·99

0·01

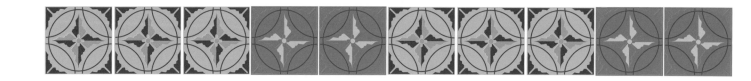

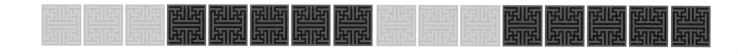

Patsy Etheridge
14 Gleneagle Road
Windy Lane
Gloschester
GL12 8BB

Wentworth Smudgitt
Deliah Close
Biggleswade
Bedfordshire
Bl4 3FT

Suzie Kettle
Teapot Street
The Tapps
Glasgow
GL7 1GG

John Bear
Wood Lane
Herts
H11 4HJ

Gerald Barks
Dashid Crescent
Liverpool
Li3 8JG

Patsy Etheridge
14 Gleneagle Road
Windy Lane
Gloschester
GL12 8BB

Patsy Etheridge
14 Gleneagle Road
Windy Lane
Gloschester
GL12 8BB

Leo has 3 computer games for every 2 that William has.
If Leo has 15 computer games, how many games does William have?

2 bananas cost 40p.
What is the cost of 3 bananas?

For every £5 that Ceri saves, her mother gives her another £1.
How much must Ceri save for her mother to give her £6?

To make a meringue you need 50g of sugar for every 1 egg white.
How much sugar would you need for 3 egg whites?

For every 15 minutes of homework Connor does, he is allowed to play on his computer for 5 minutes.
If Connor does 1 hour's homework, how long is he allowed to spend on his computer?

10 minutes out of every 1 hour of a maths lesson is spent on mental maths.
How much time is spent on mental maths in 5 hours of maths lessons?

Mum is going to buy 2 litres of juice for every 5 children at a birthday party.
If there are 15 children coming to the party, how much juice will she buy?

Here are the ingredients to make
20 chocolate chip cookies.
Change the weights to make 30 cookies.

Chocolate chip cookies
60g butter
100g flour
60g sugar
50g chocolate chips

In every 1 packet of
chocolates, there are
6 white chocolates.
How many white
chocolates are there
in 5 packets?

The Supermarket has a
special offer. You get 10p
back for every £10 you spend.
How much would you get
back if you spent £60?

Paul has made a pattern out of mosaic
tiles using two different colours.
2 in every 3 tiles are yellow.
If there are 18 tiles in the pattern, how
many are yellow?

For every 5 bars of Mighty
Fibre you buy, you get 2
superhero cards.
How many bars of Mighty
Fibre do you need to buy
to get all 10 cards?

A recipe for 2 people needs
120 ml of cream.
How many millilitres of cream
are needed for 8 people?

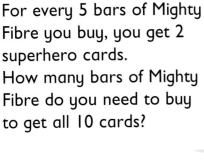

Number facts for 0

0 + 0 = 0	0 − 0 = 0

Number facts for 1

1 + 0 = 1	1 − 0 = 1
0 + 1 = 1	1 − 1 = 0

Number facts for 2

2 + 0 = 2	2 − 0 = 2
1 + 1 = 2	2 − 1 = 1
0 + 2 = 2	2 − 2 = 0

Number facts for 3

3 + 0 = 3	3 − 0 = 3
2 + 1 = 3	3 − 1 = 2
1 + 2 = 3	3 − 2 = 1
0 + 3 = 3	3 − 3 = 0

Number facts for 4

4 + 0 = 4	4 − 0 = 4
3 + 1 = 4	4 − 1 = 3
2 + 2 = 4	4 − 2 = 2
1 + 3 = 4	4 − 3 = 1
0 + 4 = 4	4 − 4 = 0

Number facts for 5

5 + 0 = 5	5 − 0 = 5
4 + 1 = 5	5 − 1 = 4
3 + 2 = 5	5 − 2 = 3
2 + 3 = 5	5 − 3 = 2
1 + 4 = 5	5 − 4 = 1
0 + 5 = 5	5 − 5 = 0

Number facts for 6

6 + 0 = 6	6 − 0 = 6
5 + 1 = 6	6 − 1 = 5
4 + 2 = 6	6 − 2 = 4
3 + 3 = 6	6 − 3 = 3
2 + 4 = 6	6 − 4 = 2
1 + 5 = 6	6 − 5 = 1
0 + 6 = 6	6 − 6 = 0

Number facts for 7

7 + 0 = 7	7 − 0 = 7
6 + 1 = 7	7 − 1 = 6
5 + 2 = 7	7 − 2 = 5
4 + 3 = 7	7 − 3 = 4
3 + 4 = 7	7 − 4 = 3
2 + 5 = 7	7 − 5 = 2
1 + 6 = 7	7 − 6 = 1
0 + 7 = 7	7 − 7 = 0

Number facts for 8

8 + 0 = 8	8 − 0 = 8
7 + 1 = 8	8 − 1 = 7
6 + 2 = 8	8 − 2 = 6
5 + 3 = 8	8 − 3 = 5
4 + 4 = 8	8 − 4 = 4
3 + 5 = 8	8 − 5 = 3
2 + 6 = 8	8 − 6 = 2
1 + 7 = 8	8 − 7 = 1
0 + 8 = 8	8 − 8 = 0

Number facts for 9

9 + 0 = 9	9 − 0 = 9
8 + 1 = 9	9 − 1 = 8
7 + 2 = 9	9 − 2 = 7
6 + 3 = 9	9 − 3 = 6
5 + 4 = 9	9 − 4 = 5
4 + 5 = 9	9 − 5 = 4
3 + 6 = 9	9 − 6 = 3
2 + 7 = 9	9 − 7 = 2
1 + 8 = 9	9 − 8 = 1
0 + 9 = 9	9 − 9 = 0

Number facts for 10

10 + 0 = 10	10 − 0 = 10
9 + 1 = 10	10 − 1 = 9
8 + 2 = 10	10 − 2 = 8
7 + 3 = 10	10 − 3 = 7
6 + 4 = 10	10 − 4 = 6
5 + 5 = 10	10 − 5 = 5
4 + 6 = 10	10 − 6 = 4
3 + 7 = 10	10 − 7 = 3
2 + 8 = 10	10 − 8 = 2
1 + 9 = 10	10 − 9 = 1
0 + 10 = 10	10 − 10 = 0

Number facts for 11

11 + 0 = 11	11 − 0 = 11
10 + 1 = 11	11 − 1 = 10
9 + 2 = 11	11 − 2 = 9
8 + 3 = 11	11 − 3 = 8
7 + 4 = 11	11 − 4 = 7
6 + 5 = 11	11 − 5 = 6
5 + 6 = 11	11 − 6 = 5
4 + 7 = 11	11 − 7 = 4
3 + 8 = 11	11 − 8 = 3
2 + 9 = 11	11 − 9 = 2
1 + 10 = 11	11 − 10 = 1
0 + 11 = 11	11 − 11 = 0

Number facts for 12

12 + 0 = 12	12 − 0 = 12
11 + 1 = 12	12 − 1 = 11
10 + 2 = 12	12 − 2 = 10
9 + 3 = 12	12 − 3 = 9
8 + 4 = 12	12 − 4 = 8
7 + 5 = 12	12 − 5 = 7
6 + 6 = 12	12 − 6 = 6
5 + 7 = 12	12 − 7 = 5
4 + 8 = 12	12 − 8 = 4
3 + 9 = 12	12 − 9 = 3
2 + 10 = 12	12 − 10 = 2
1 + 11 = 12	12 − 11 = 1
0 + 12 = 12	12 − 12 = 0

Number facts for 13

13 + 0 = 13	13 − 0 = 13
12 + 1 = 13	13 − 1 = 12
11 + 2 = 13	13 − 2 = 11
10 + 3 = 13	13 − 3 = 10
9 + 4 = 13	13 − 4 = 9
8 + 5 = 13	13 − 5 = 8
7 + 6 = 13	13 − 6 = 7
6 + 7 = 13	13 − 7 = 6
5 + 8 = 13	13 − 8 = 5
4 + 9 = 13	13 − 9 = 4
3 + 10 = 13	13 − 10 = 3
2 + 11 = 13	13 − 11 = 2
1 + 12 = 13	13 − 12 = 1
0 + 13 = 13	13 − 13 = 0

Number facts for 14

14 + 0 = 14	14 − 0 = 14
13 + 1 = 14	14 − 1 = 13
12 + 2 = 14	14 − 2 = 12
11 + 3 = 14	14 − 3 = 11
10 + 4 = 14	14 − 4 = 10
9 + 5 = 14	14 − 5 = 9
8 + 6 = 14	14 − 6 = 8
7 + 7 = 14	14 − 7 = 7
6 + 8 = 14	14 − 8 = 6
5 + 9 = 14	14 − 9 = 5
4 + 10 = 14	14 − 10 = 4
3 + 11 = 14	14 − 11 = 3
2 + 12 = 14	14 − 12 = 2
1 + 13 = 14	14 − 13 = 1
0 + 14 = 14	14 − 14 = 0

Number facts for 15

15 + 0 = 15	15 − 0 = 15
14 + 1 = 15	15 − 1 = 14
13 + 2 = 15	15 − 2 = 13
12 + 3 = 15	15 − 3 = 12
11 + 4 = 15	15 − 4 = 11
10 + 5 = 15	15 − 5 = 10
9 + 6 = 15	15 − 6 = 9
8 + 7 = 15	15 − 7 = 8
7 + 8 = 15	15 − 8 = 7
6 + 9 = 15	15 − 9 = 6
5 + 10 = 15	15 − 10 = 5
4 + 11 = 15	15 − 11 = 4
3 + 12 = 15	15 − 12 = 3
2 + 13 = 15	15 − 13 = 2
1 + 14 = 15	15 − 14 = 1
0 + 15 = 15	15 − 15 = 0

Number facts for 16

16 + 0 = 16	16 − 0 = 16
15 + 1 = 16	16 − 1 = 15
14 + 2 = 16	16 − 2 = 14
13 + 3 = 16	16 − 3 = 13
12 + 4 = 16	16 − 4 = 12
11 + 5 = 16	16 − 5 = 11
10 + 6 = 16	16 − 6 = 10
9 + 7 = 16	16 − 7 = 9
8 + 8 = 16	16 − 8 = 8
7 + 9 = 16	16 − 9 = 7
6 + 10 = 16	16 − 10 = 6
5 + 11 = 16	16 − 11 = 5
4 + 12 = 16	16 − 12 = 4
3 + 13 = 16	16 − 13 = 3
2 + 14 = 16	16 − 14 = 2
1 + 15 = 16	16 − 15 = 1
0 + 16 = 16	16 − 16 = 0

Number facts for 17

17 + 0 = 17	17 − 0 = 17
16 + 1 = 17	17 − 1 = 16
15 + 2 = 17	17 − 2 = 15
14 + 3 = 17	17 − 3 = 14
13 + 4 = 17	17 − 4 = 13
12 + 5 = 17	17 − 5 = 12
11 + 6 = 17	17 − 6 = 11
10 + 7 = 17	17 − 7 = 10
9 + 8 = 17	17 − 8 = 9
8 + 9 = 17	17 − 9 = 8
7 + 10 = 17	17 − 10 = 7
6 + 11 = 17	17 − 11 = 6
5 + 12 = 17	17 − 12 = 5
4 + 13 = 17	17 − 13 = 4
3 + 14 = 17	17 − 14 = 3
2 + 15 = 17	17 − 15 = 2
1 + 16 = 17	17 − 16 = 1
0 + 17 = 17	17 − 17 = 0

Number facts for 18

18 + 0 = 18	18 − 0 = 18
17 + 1 = 18	18 − 1 = 17
16 + 2 = 18	18 − 2 = 16
15 + 3 = 18	18 − 3 = 15
14 + 4 = 18	18 − 4 = 14
13 + 5 = 18	18 − 5 = 13
12 + 6 = 18	18 − 6 = 12
11 + 7 = 18	18 − 7 = 11
10 + 8 = 18	18 − 8 = 10
9 + 9 = 18	18 − 9 = 9
8 + 10 = 18	18 − 10 = 8
7 + 11 = 18	18 − 11 = 7
6 + 12 = 18	18 − 12 = 6
5 + 13 = 18	18 − 13 = 5
4 + 14 = 18	18 − 14 = 4
3 + 15 = 18	18 − 15 = 3
2 + 16 = 18	18 − 16 = 2
1 + 17 = 18	18 − 17 = 1
0 + 18 = 18	18 − 18 = 0

Number facts for 19

19 + 0 = 19	19 − 0 = 19
18 + 1 = 19	19 − 1 = 18
17 + 2 = 19	19 − 2 = 17
16 + 3 = 19	19 − 3 = 16
15 + 4 = 19	19 − 4 = 15
14 + 5 = 19	19 − 5 = 14
13 + 6 = 19	19 − 6 = 13
12 + 7 = 19	19 − 7 = 12
11 + 8 = 19	19 − 8 = 11
10 + 9 = 19	19 − 9 = 10
9 + 10 = 19	19 − 10 = 9
8 + 11 = 19	19 − 11 = 8
7 + 12 = 19	19 − 12 = 7
6 + 13 = 19	19 − 13 = 6
5 + 14 = 19	19 − 14 = 5
4 + 15 = 19	19 − 15 = 4
3 + 16 = 19	19 − 16 = 3
2 + 17 = 19	19 − 17 = 2
1 + 18 = 19	19 − 18 = 1
0 + 19 = 19	19 − 19 = 0

Number facts for 20

20 + 0 = 20	20 − 0 = 20
19 + 1 = 20	20 − 1 = 19
18 + 2 = 20	20 − 2 = 18
17 + 3 = 20	20 − 3 = 17
16 + 4 = 20	20 − 4 = 16
15 + 5 = 20	20 − 5 = 15
14 + 6 = 20	20 − 6 = 14
13 + 7 = 20	20 − 7 = 13
12 + 8 = 20	20 − 8 = 12
11 + 9 = 20	20 − 9 = 11
10 + 10 = 20	20 − 10 = 10
9 + 11 = 20	20 − 11 = 9
8 + 12 = 20	20 − 12 = 8
7 + 13 = 20	20 − 13 = 7
6 + 14 = 20	20 − 14 = 6
5 + 15 = 20	20 − 15 = 5
4 + 16 = 20	20 − 16 = 4
3 + 17 = 20	20 − 17 = 3
2 + 18 = 20	20 − 18 = 2
1 + 19 = 20	20 − 19 = 1
0 + 20 = 20	20 − 20 = 0

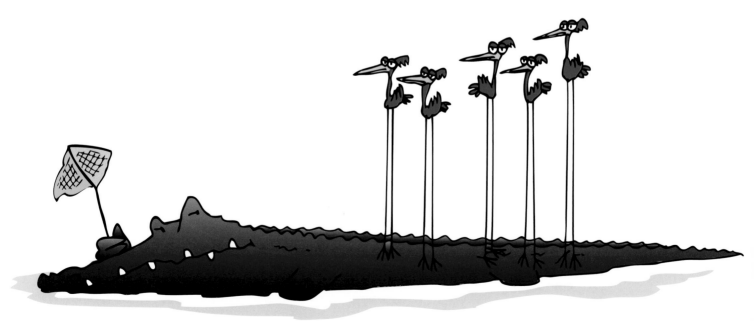

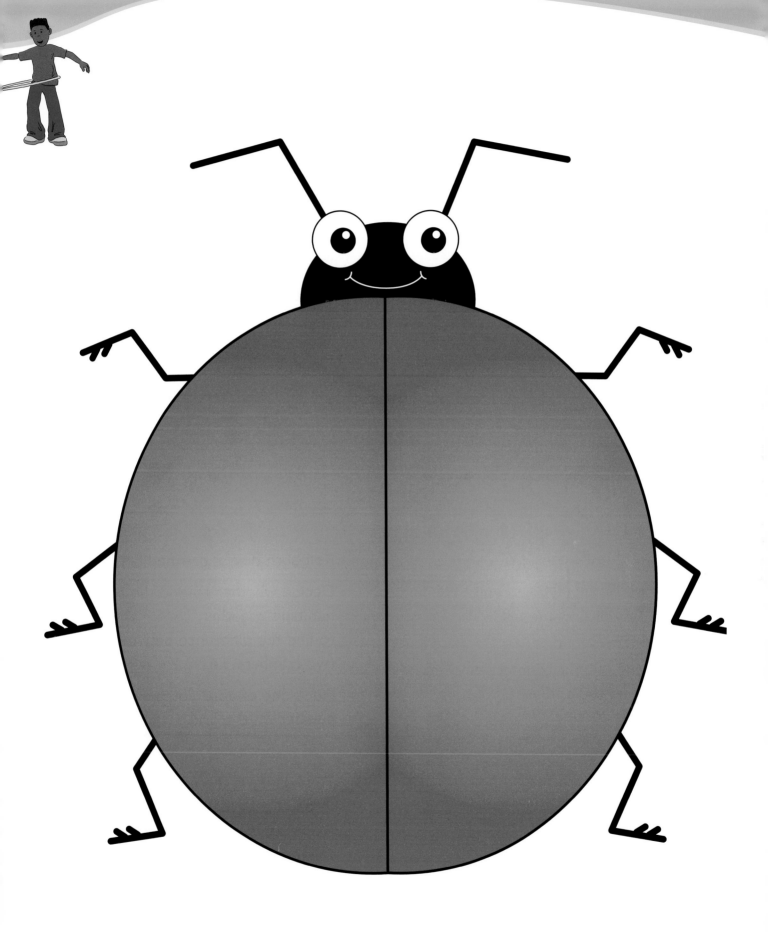

Add and subtract the dice

A game for 2 players

You need:
- three 1–6 dice
- counters in two different colours

Before you start:
- Choose who will have which colour counters.

Take turns to:
- Roll the three dice, e.g. 5, 2 and 6.
- Add two of the numbers and take away the third, e.g. 5 + 6 = 11, 11 − 2 = 9.
- Place one of your counters on that number on the grid.

The winner is the first player to get three of their counters in a line. A line can be along a row or a column or a diagonal.

Add or subtract the dice

A game for 2 players

You need:
- two 0–9 dice
- counters in two different colours

Before you start:
- Choose who will have which colour counters.

Take turns to:
- Roll both dice, e.g. 4 and 8.
- Decide whether to add the two numbers together, i.e. 4 + 8 = 12, or to find the difference between the two numbers, i.e. 8 − 4 = 4.
- Place one of your counters on that number on the grid.

The winner is the first player to get three of their counters in a line. A line can be along a row or a column or a diagonal.

6	10	4	12	7	11	3	14
6	13	9	16	8	14	5	9
8	15	10	7	4	5	11	7
17	12	9	10	13	8	11	2
18	1	0	12	4	7	15	16
12	4	10	6	8	2	9	6
3	5	1	11	12	9	7	8
13	11	14	10	5	17	0	18

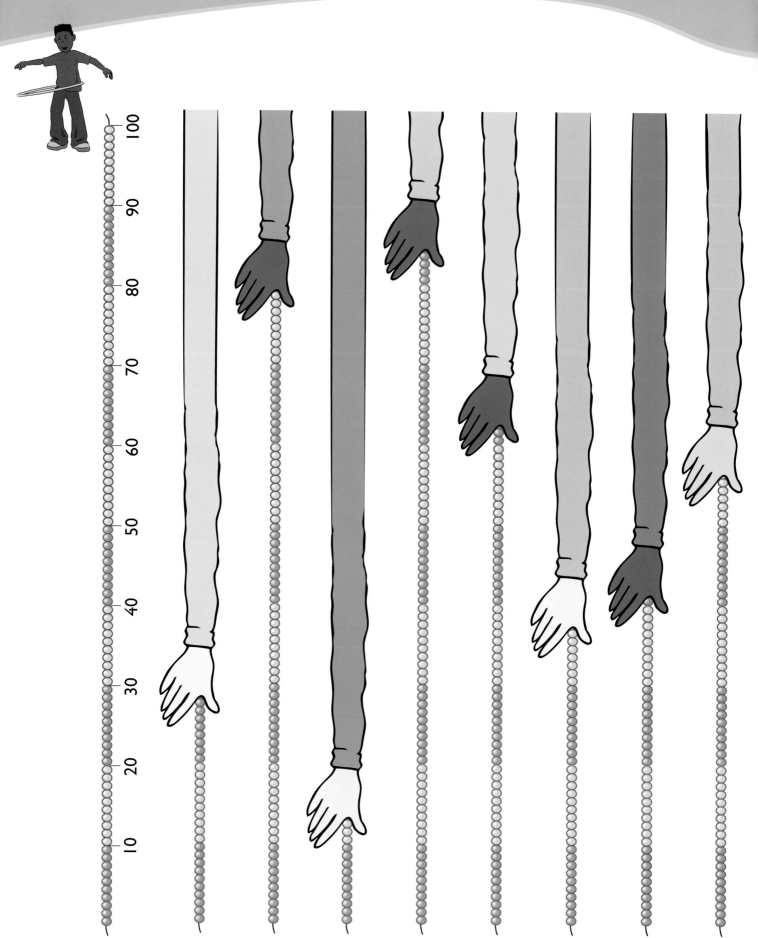

48 + 7 = 55

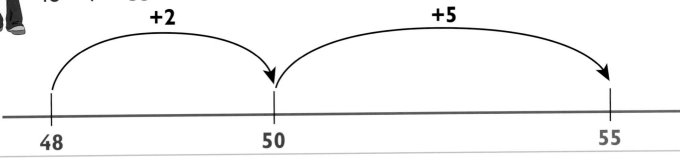

63 + 8 = 71

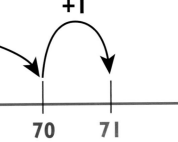

Remember

- Addition can be done in any order, e.g. 78 + 86 is the same as 86 + 78.
- Put the larger number first.
- Count on the number of tens in the smaller number.
- Count on the number of units in the smaller number.

65 + 47 = 112

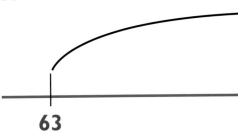

OR

78 + 86 = 164

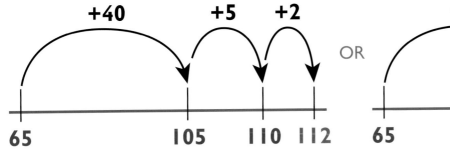

OR

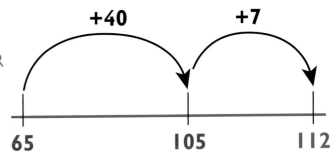

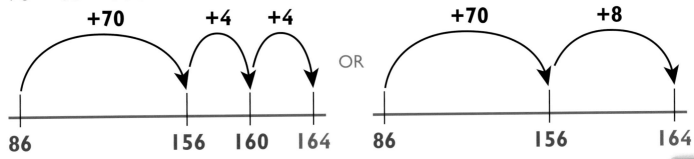

Remember

You can work out the answer to a subtraction calculation by:
- counting back (take away) or
- counting up (find the difference).

83 – 6 = 77

- counting back
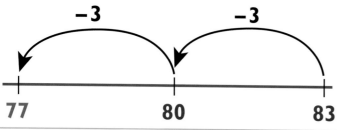

- counting up
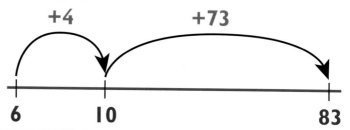

62 – 8 = 54

- counting back
- counting up
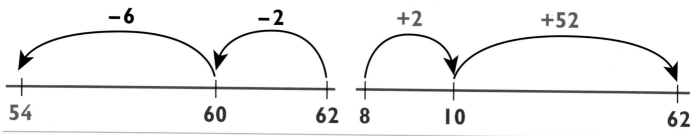

85 – 37 = 48

- counting back
- counting up
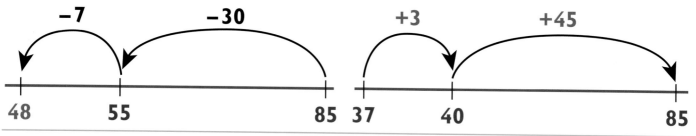

72 – 45 = 27

- counting back
- counting up
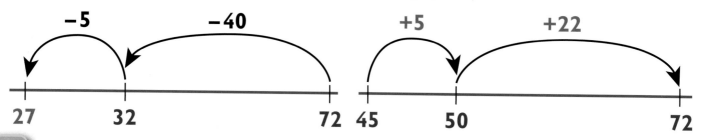

Remember

● Addition can be done in any order, e.g. 2·8 + 7·5 is the same as 7·5 + 2·8.

● Put the larger number first.

● Count on the number of units in the smaller number.

● Count on the number of tenths in the smaller number.

6·7 + 4·6 = 11·3

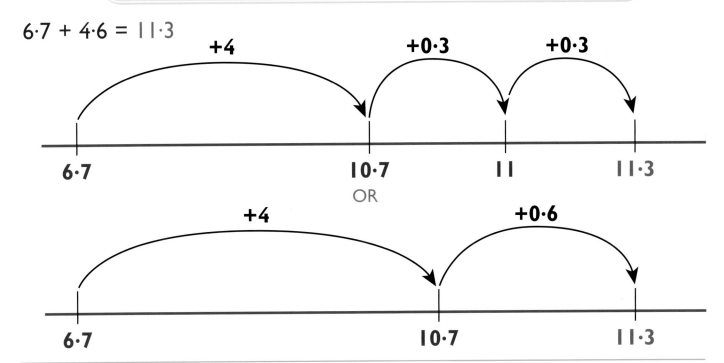

2·8 + 7·5 = 10·3

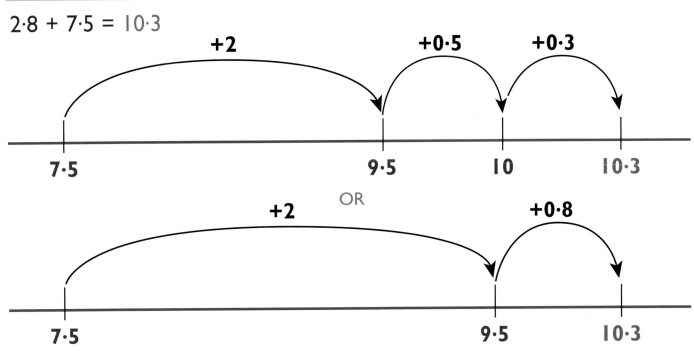

6·5 − 2·7 = 3·8
- counting back

- counting up

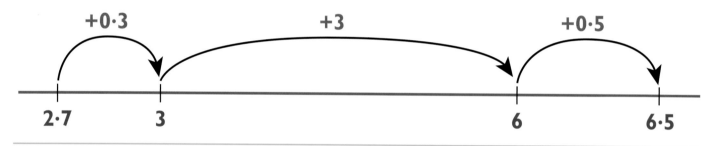

8·2 − 5·6 = 2·6
- counting back

- counting up

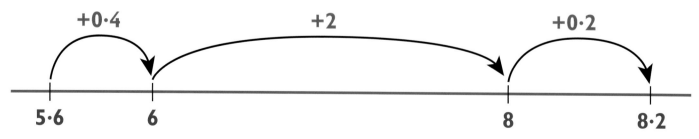

Written methods for addition of whole numbers

Partitioning

63 + 78

```
    60  +  3
+   70  +  8
   130  + 11  = 141
```

486 + 367

```
   400  +  80  +  6
+  300  +  60  +  7
   700  + 140  + 13  = 853
```

68 + 78

Expanded method

Adding the most significant digit first

```
   63
+  78
  130
   11
  141
```

Adding the least significant digit first

```
   63
+  78
   11
  130
  141
```

Column method

```
   63
+  78
  141
   1
```

486 + 367

Expanded method

Adding the most significant digit first

```
   486
+  367
   700
   140
    13
   853
```

Adding the least significant digit first

```
   486
+  367
    13
   140
   700
   853
```

Column method

```
   486
+  367
   853
   1 1
```

Other examples using the column method

675 + 87

```
   675
+   87
   762
   1 1
```

509 + 68

```
   509
+   68
   577
    1
```

47 + 156 + 861

```
    47
   156
+  861
  1064
   1 1
```

465 + 205 + 184

```
   465
   205
+  184
   854
   1 1
```

Written methods for subtraction of whole numbers

The counting up method

76 − 47

```
   76
 − 47
    3  (→ 50)
   20  (→ 70)
    6  (→ 76)
   29
```

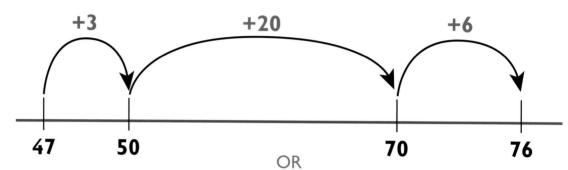

OR

```
   76
 − 47
    3  (→ 50)
   26  (→ 76)
   29
```

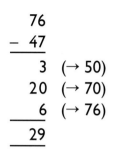
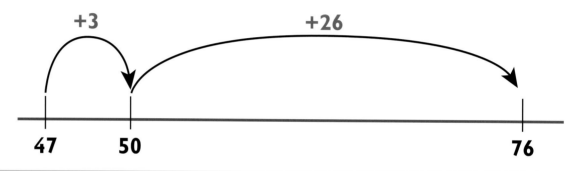

542 − 267

```
   542
 − 267
     3  (→ 270)
    30  (→ 300)
   200  (→ 500)
    40  (→ 540)
     2  (→ 542)
   275
```

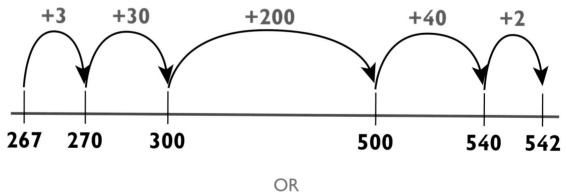

OR

```
   542
 − 267
    33  (→ 300)
   242  (→ 542)
   275
```

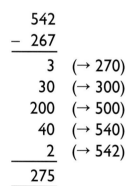
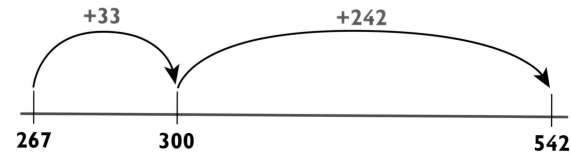

76 − 47

Expanded method

70 + 6
− 40 + 7

⁶⁰ ¹⁶
7̶0̶ + 6̶
− 40 + 7
20 + 9   = 29

Column method

^{6 16}
7̶6
− 47
29

865 − 243

Expanded method

800 + 60 + 5
− 200 + 40 + 3

800 + 60 + 5
− 200 + 40 + 3
600 + 20 + 2   = 622

Column method

865
− 243
622

637 − 484

Expanded method

600 + 30 + 7
− 400 + 80 + 4

⁵⁰⁰   ¹³⁰
6̶0̶0̶ + 3̶0̶ + 7
− 400 + 80 + 4
100 + 50 + 3   = 153

Column method

^{5 13}
6̶3̶7
− 484
153

542 − 267

Expanded method

500 + 40 + 2
− 200 + 60 + 7

⁴⁰⁰   ¹³⁰   ¹²
^{5̶0̶0̶}   ^{3̶0̶}   12
5̶0̶0̶ + 4̶0̶ + 2̶
− 200 + 60 + 7
200 + 70 + 5   = 275

Column method

^{4 13 12}
5̶4̶2̶
− 267
275

504 − 368

Expanded method

500 + 0 + 4
− 300 + 60 + 8

⁴⁰⁰   ⁹⁰   ¹⁴
⁴⁰⁰   ^{1̶0̶0̶}   4
5̶0̶0̶ + 0̶ + 4
− 300 + 60 + 8
100 + 30 + 6   = 136

Column method

^{4 9 14}
5̶0̶4̶
− 368
136

Written methods for addition of decimals

Partitioning

8·36 + 4·78

```
    8 + 0·3 + 0·06
  + 4 + 0·7 + 0·08
  ──────────────────
   12 + 1·0 + 0·14  = 13.14
```

27·58 + 45·63

```
   20 +  7 + 0·5 + 0·08
 + 40 +  5 + 0·6 + 0·03
 ──────────────────────
   60 + 12 + 1·1 + 0·11  = 73·21
```

8·36 + 4·78

Expanded method

Adding the most significant digit first

```
   8·36
 + 4·78
 ───────
  12·00
   1·00
   0·14
 ───────
  13·14
```

Adding the least significant digit first

```
   8·36
 + 4·78
 ───────
   0·14
   1·00
  12·00
 ───────
  13·14
```

Column method

```
   8·36
 + 4·78
 ───────
  13·14
   1 1
```

27·58 + 45·63

Expanded method

Adding the most significant digit first

```
  27·58
+ 45·63
────────
  60·00
  12·00
   1·10
   0·11
────────
  73·21
```

Adding the least significant digit first

```
  27·58
+ 45·63
────────
   0·11
   1·10
  12·00
  60·00
────────
  73·21
```

Column method

```
  27·58
+ 45·63
────────
  73·21
   1 1
```

Other examples using the column method

55·7 + 26·4

```
   55·7
 + 26·4
 ───────
   82·1
    1 1
```

34·7 + 28·51

```
  34·70
+ 28·51
────────
  63·21
    1 1
```

15·08 + 9·64 + 8·7

```
  15·08
   9·64
+  8·70
────────
  33·42
   2 1 1
```

Written methods for subtraction of decimals

8·75 − 3·87

Expanded method

$$
\begin{array}{r}
8 + 0.7 + 0.05 \\
-\ 3 + 0.8 + 0.07 \\
\hline
\end{array}
$$

$$
\begin{array}{ccc}
7 & 1\cdot60 & 0\cdot15 \\
\cancel{8} & \cancel{0\cdot6} & 0\cdot15 \\
\end{array}
$$
$$
\begin{array}{r}
\cancel{8} + \cancel{0.7} + \cancel{0.05} \\
-\ 3 + 0.8 + 0.07 \\
\hline
4 + 0.8 + 0.08 = 4\cdot88 \\
\end{array}
$$

Column method

$$
\begin{array}{r}
{}^{7}\ {}^{16}\ {}^{15} \\
8\cdot7\cancel{5} \\
-\ 3\cdot87 \\
\hline
4\cdot88 \\
\end{array}
$$

72·6 − 43·9

Expanded method

$$
\begin{array}{r}
70 + 2 + 0.6 \\
-\ 40 + 3 + 0.9 \\
\hline
\end{array}
$$

$$
\begin{array}{ccc}
60 & 11 & 1\cdot6 \\
\cancel{70} & + & 1\cdot6 \\
\end{array}
$$
$$
\begin{array}{r}
\cancel{70} + \cancel{2} + \cancel{0.6} \\
-\ 40 + 3 + 0.9 \\
\hline
20 + 8 + 0.7 = 28\cdot7 \\
\end{array}
$$

Column method

$$
\begin{array}{r}
{}^{6}\ {}^{11}\ {}^{16} \\
7\cancel{2}\cdot\cancel{6} \\
-\ 43\cdot9 \\
\hline
28\cdot7 \\
\end{array}
$$

85·43 − 46·54

Expanded method

$$
\begin{array}{r}
80 + 5 + 0.4 + 0.03 \\
-\ 40 + 6 + 0.5 + 0.04 \\
\hline
\end{array}
$$

$$
\begin{array}{cccc}
70 & 14 & 1\cdot3 & 0\cdot13 \\
\cancel{80} & \cancel{4} & 1\cdot3 & 0\cdot13 \\
80 & \cancel{5} & \cancel{0\cdot3} & 0\cdot13 \\
\end{array}
$$
$$
\begin{array}{r}
\cancel{80} + \cancel{5} + \cancel{0.4} + \cancel{0.03} \\
-\ 40 + 6 + 0.5 + 0.04 \\
\hline
30 + 8 + 0.8 + 0.09 = 38\cdot89 \\
\end{array}
$$

Column method

$$
\begin{array}{r}
{}^{7}\ {}^{14}\ {}^{13}\ {}^{13} \\
8\cancel{5}\cdot\cancel{43} \\
-\ 46\cdot54 \\
\hline
38\cdot89 \\
\end{array}
$$

Written methods for subtraction of decimals

The counting up method

8·75 − 3·87

```
  8·75
− 3·87
───────
  0·03   (→ 3·9)
  0·10   (→ 4)
  4·00   (→ 8)
  0·75   (→ 8·75)
───────
  4·88
```

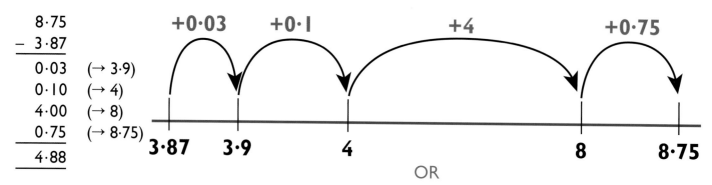

OR

```
  8·75
− 3·87
───────
  0·13   (→ 4)
  4·75   (→ 8·75)
───────
  4·88
```

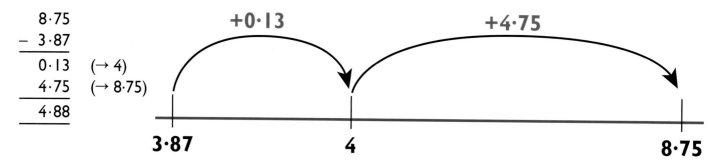

72·6 − 43·9

```
  72·6
− 43.9
───────
  0·1    (→ 44)
 28·0    (→ 72)
  0·6    (→ 72·6)
───────
 28·7
```

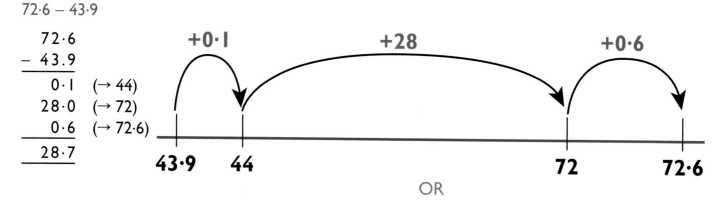

OR

```
  72·6
− 43.9
───────
  0·1    (→ 44)
 28·6    (→ 72·6)
───────
 28·7
```

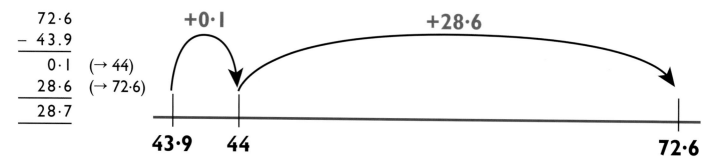

85·43 − 46·54

```
  85·43
− 46·54
   0·06   (→ 46·6)
   0·40   (→ 47)
  38·00   (→ 85)
   0·43   (→ 85·43)
  38·89
```

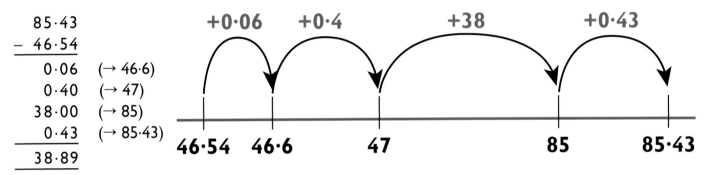

```
  85·43
− 46·54
   0·46   (→ 47)
  38·43   (→ 85·43)
  38·89
```

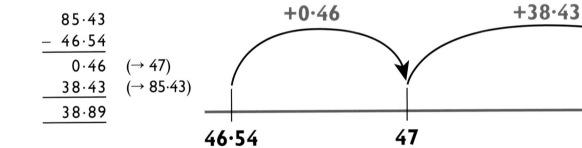

The multiplication game

A game for 2 players

You need:
- two 0–9 dice
- counters in two different colours

Before you start:
- Choose who will have which colour counters.

Take turns to:
- Roll both dice.
- Multiply the two numbers together.
- Place one of your counters on that number on the grid.

The winner is the first player to get 3 of their counters in a line. A line can be along a row or a column or a diagonal.

The multiples game

A game for 2 players

You need:
- 0–9 dice
- counters in two different colours

Before you start:
- Choose who will have which colour counters.

Take turns to:
- Roll the dice.
- Find a number on the grid that is a multiple of the dice number.
- Place one of your counters on that number on the grid.

Rule:
- If you roll a 0 or a 1, roll the dice again.

The winner is the first player to get 3 of their counters in a line. A line can be along a row or a column or a diagonal.

The division game

A game for 2 players

You need:
- 0–9 dice
- 20 counters:
  10 of one colour,
  10 of another

Before you start:
- Choose who will have which colour counters.
- Take turns to place one of your counters on a number on the grid, until all 20 counters are on the grid.

Take turns to:
- Roll the dice.
- If one of the numbers you have covered on the grid can be divided exactly by the dice number, remove that counter from the grid.

Rules:
- If you roll a 0 or a 1, roll the dice again.
- You can only remove one counter from the grid each turn.

The winner is the first player to remove their 10 counters.

35	2	1	32	12	28	9	4	5
6	48	8	16	20	2	56	24	6
12	10	25	4	56	30	40	7	72
24	3	49	14	21	6	27	14	3
0	8	24	18	40	16	9	63	54
42	21	6	42	12	48	10	36	81
16	32	12	35	15	30	54	45	9
45	18	36	28	63	24	18	4	8
5	15	7	64	8	18	20	36	27

52 × 6

300p   12p

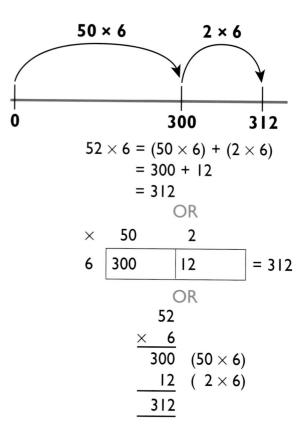

50 × 6   2 × 6

0   300   312

52 × 6 = (50 × 6) + (2 × 6)
= 300 + 12
= 312

OR

×	50	2	
6	300	12	= 312

OR

```
    52
×    6
   300   (50 × 6)
    12   ( 2 × 6)
   312
```

76 × 4

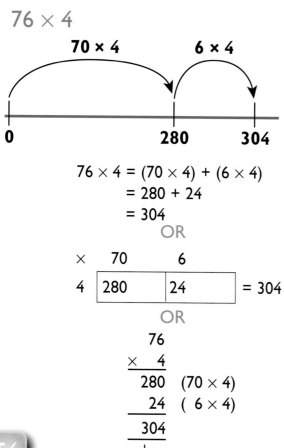

70 × 4   6 × 4

0   280   304

76 × 4 = (70 × 4) + (6 × 4)
= 280 + 24
= 304

OR

×	70	6	
4	280	24	= 304

OR

```
    76
×    4
   280   (70 × 4)
    24   ( 6 × 4)
   304
     1
```

43 × 8

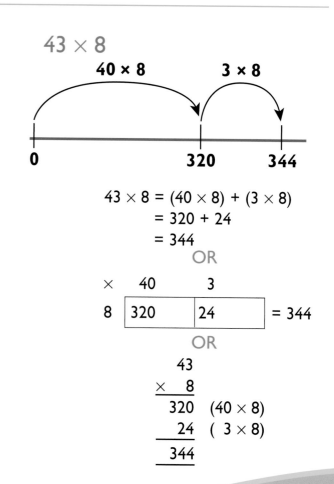

40 × 8   3 × 8

0   320   344

43 × 8 = (40 × 8) + (3 × 8)
= 320 + 24
= 344

OR

×	40	3	
8	320	24	= 344

OR

```
    43
×    8
   320   (40 × 8)
    24   ( 3 × 8)
   344
```

Written methods for multiplication of whole numbers

Partitioning

53 × 8

53 × 8 = (50 × 8) + (3 × 8)
       = 400 + 24
       = 424

324 × 6

324 × 6 = (300 × 6) + (20 × 6) + (4 × 6)
        = 1800 + 120 + 24
        = 1944

53 × 8

Grid method

×	50	3	
8	400	24	= 424

Expanded method

```
    53
×    8
   400   (50 × 8)
    24   ( 3 × 8)
   424
```

Short multiplication

```
    53
×    8
   424
    2
```

324 × 6

Grid method

×	300	20	4	
6	1800	120	24	= 1944

Expanded method

```
    324
×     6
   1800   (300 × 6)
    120   ( 20 × 6)
     24   (  4 × 6)
   1944
```

Short multiplication

```
    324
×     6
   1944
    1 2
```

59 × 74

Grid method

×	50	9	
70	3500	630	4130
4	200	36	236
			4366

Expanded method

```
     59
×    74
   3500   (50 × 70)
    630   ( 9 × 70)
    200   (50 ×  4)
     36   ( 9 ×  4)
   4366
    1
```

Reduced to

```
     59
×    74
   4130   (59 × 70)
    236   (59 ×  4)
   4366
```

Written methods for division of whole numbers

83 ÷ 5

Partitioning

$83 ÷ 5 = (50 ÷ 5) + (33 ÷ 5)$
$= 10 + 6 \text{ R } 3$
$= 16 \text{ R } 3$

Expanded method

$$5\overline{)\ \ 83}$$
$$-\ 50 \quad (5 × 10)$$
$$\overline{\ \ 33}$$
$$-\ 30 \quad (5 × \underline{6})$$
$$\overline{\ \ \ 3}$$

Answer: 16 R 3

Short division

$$\begin{array}{r} 10 +\ \ 6 \text{ R } 3 \\ \hline 5\overline{)\ 50 + 33} \end{array}$$

Reduced to

$$\begin{array}{r} 1\ \ 6 \text{ R } 3 \\ \hline 5\overline{)\ 8^3 3} \end{array}$$

---

97 ÷ 4

Partitioning

$97 ÷ 4 = (80 ÷ 4) + (17 ÷ 4)$
$= 20 + 4 \text{ R } 1$
$= 24 \text{ R } 1$

Expanded method

$$4\overline{)\ \ 97}$$
$$-\ 40 \quad (4 × 10)$$
$$\overline{\ \ 57}$$
$$-\ 40 \quad (4 × 10)$$
$$\overline{\ \ 17}$$
$$-\ 16 \quad (4 × \underline{4})$$
$$\overline{\ \ \ 1}$$

Answer: 24 R 1

Reduced to

$$4\overline{)\ \ 97}$$
$$-\ 80 \quad (4 × 20)$$
$$\overline{\ \ 17}$$
$$-\ 16 \quad (4 × \underline{4})$$
$$\overline{\ \ \ 1}$$

Answer: 24 R 1

Short division

$$\begin{array}{r} 20 +\ \ 4 \text{ R } 1 \\ \hline 4\overline{)\ 80 + 17} \end{array}$$

Reduced to

$$\begin{array}{r} 2\ 4 \text{ R } 1 \\ \hline 4\overline{)\ 9^1 7} \end{array}$$

167 ÷ 6

Expanded method

```
6) 167
  - 60   (6 × 10)
  107
  - 60   (6 × 10)
   47
  - 42   (6 × 7)
    5
```

Answer: 27 R 5

Reduced to

```
6) 167
  - 120   (6 × 20)
   47
  - 42   (6 × 7)
    5
```

Answer: 27 R 5

Short division

```
    20 +  7 R 5
6) 120 + 47
```

Reduced to

```
    2 7 R 5
6) 1 6⁴7
```

541 ÷ 7

Expanded method

```
7) 541
  - 140   (7 × 20)
  401
  - 140   (7 × 20)
  261
  - 140   (7 × 20)
  121
  - 70    (7 × 10)
   51
  - 49    (7 × 7)
    2
```

Answer: 77 R 2

Reduced to

```
7) 541
  - 490   (7 × 70)
   51
  - 49    (7 × 7)
    2
```

Answer: 77 R 2

Short division

```
    70 +  7 R 2
7) 490 + 51
```

```
    7 7 R 2
7) 5 4⁵1
```

Written methods for multiplication of decimals

3·8 × 6

Partitioning

3·8 × 6 = (3 × 6) + (0·8 × 6)
 = 18 + 4·8
 = 22·8

Grid method

×	3	0·8	
6	18	4·8	= 22·8

Expanded method

```
    3·8
 ×  6·0
 ─────
  18·0   (3   × 6)
   4·8   (0.8 × 6)
 ─────
  22·8
   1
```

Short multiplication

```
    3·8
 ×  6·0
 ─────
  22·8
    4
```

7·4 × 9

Partitioning

7·4 × 9 = (7 × 9) + (0·4 × 9)
 = 63 + 3·6
 = 66·6

Grid method

×	7	0·4	
9	63	3·6	= 66·6

Expanded method

```
    7·4
 ×  9·0
 ─────
  63·0   (7   × 9)
   3·6   (0.4 × 9)
 ─────
  66·6
```

Short multiplication

```
    7·4
 ×  9·0
 ─────
  66·6
    3
```

×	1	2	3	4	5	6	7	8	9	10
1	1	2	3	4	5	6	7	8	9	10
2	2	4	6	8	10	12	14	16	18	20
3	3	6	9	12	15	18	21	24	27	30
4	4	8	12	16	20	24	28	32	36	40
5	5	10	15	20	25	30	35	40	45	50
6	6	12	18	24	30	36	42	48	54	60
7	7	14	21	28	35	42	49	56	63	70
8	8	16	24	32	40	48	56	64	72	80
9	9	18	27	36	45	54	63	72	81	90
10	10	20	30	40	50	60	70	80	90	100

×	0·1	0·2	0·3	0·4	0·5	0·6	0·7	0·8	0·9	1
1	0·1	0·2	0·3	0·4	0·5	0·6	0·7	0·8	0·9	1
2	0·2	0·4	0·6	0·8	1	1·2	1·4	1·6	1·8	2
3	0·3	0·6	0·9	1·2	1·5	1·8	2·1	2·4	2·7	3
4	0·4	0·8	1·2	1·6	2	2·4	2·8	3·2	3·6	4
5	0·5	1	1·5	2	2·5	3	3·5	4	4·5	5
6	0·6	1·2	1·8	2·4	3	3·6	4·2	4·8	5·4	6
7	0·7	1·4	2·1	2·8	3·5	4·2	4·9	5·6	6·3	7
8	0·8	1·6	2·4	3·2	4	4·8	5·6	6·4	7·2	8
9	0·9	1·8	2·7	3·6	4·5	5·4	6·3	7·2	8·1	9
10	1	2	3	4	5	6	7	8	9	10

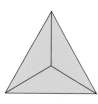

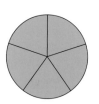

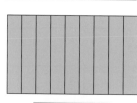

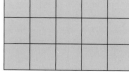

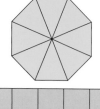

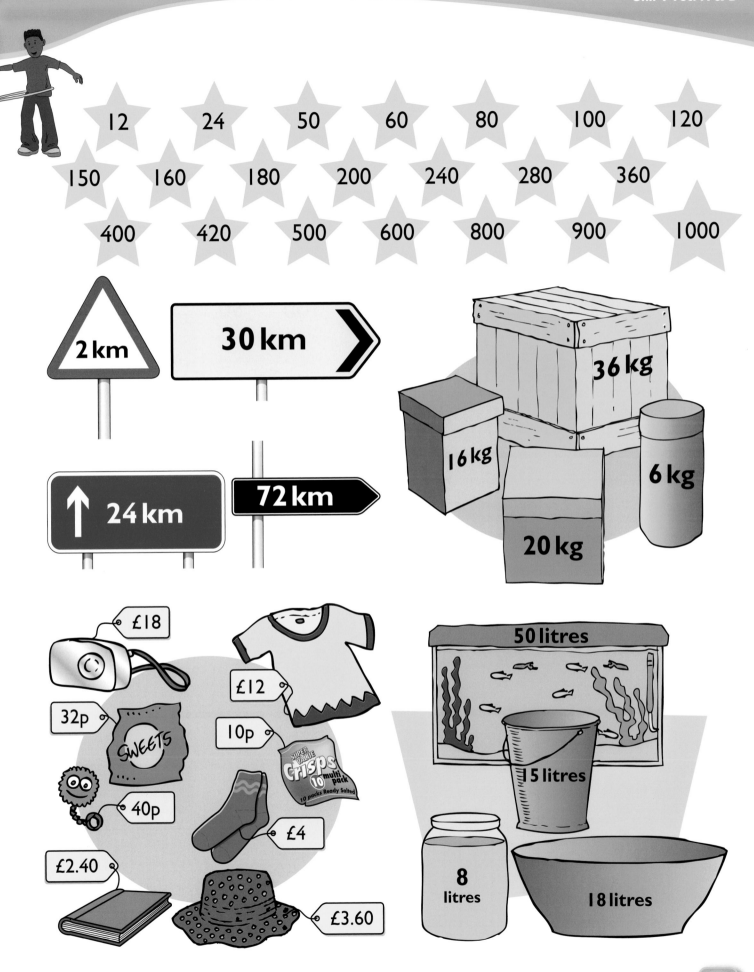

12   24   50   60   80   100   120

150   160   180   200   240   280   360

400   420   500   600   800   900   1000

2 km   30 km

24 km   72 km

36 kg

16 kg   6 kg

20 kg

£18

£12

32p

10p

SWEETS

SUPER VALUE Crisps 10 multi pack
10 packs Ready Salted

40p

£4

£2.40

£3.60

50 litres

15 litres

8 litres

18 litres

61

$\dfrac{1}{100}$

1%

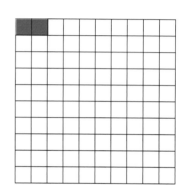

$\dfrac{2}{100}$ or $\dfrac{1}{50}$

2%

$\dfrac{5}{100}$ or $\dfrac{1}{20}$

5%

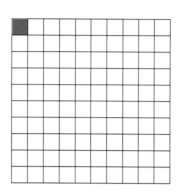

$\dfrac{10}{100}$ or $\dfrac{1}{10}$

10%

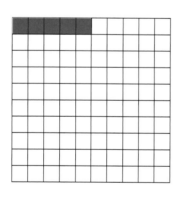

$\dfrac{20}{100}$ or $\dfrac{1}{5}$

20%

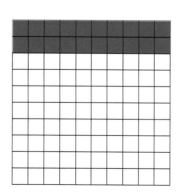

$\dfrac{25}{100}$ or $\dfrac{1}{4}$

25%

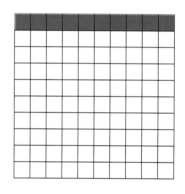

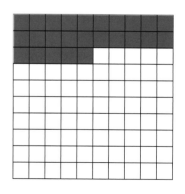

$\dfrac{40}{100}$ or $\dfrac{2}{5}$

40%

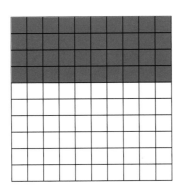

$\dfrac{50}{100}$ or $\dfrac{1}{2}$

50%

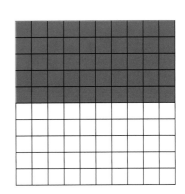

$\dfrac{70}{100}$ or $\dfrac{7}{10}$

70%

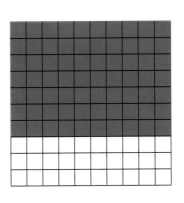

$\dfrac{75}{100}$ or $\dfrac{3}{4}$

75%

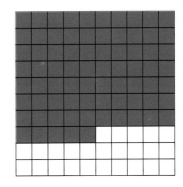

$\dfrac{80}{100}$ or $\dfrac{4}{5}$

80%

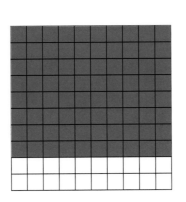

$\dfrac{100}{100}$ or 1

100%

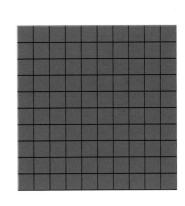

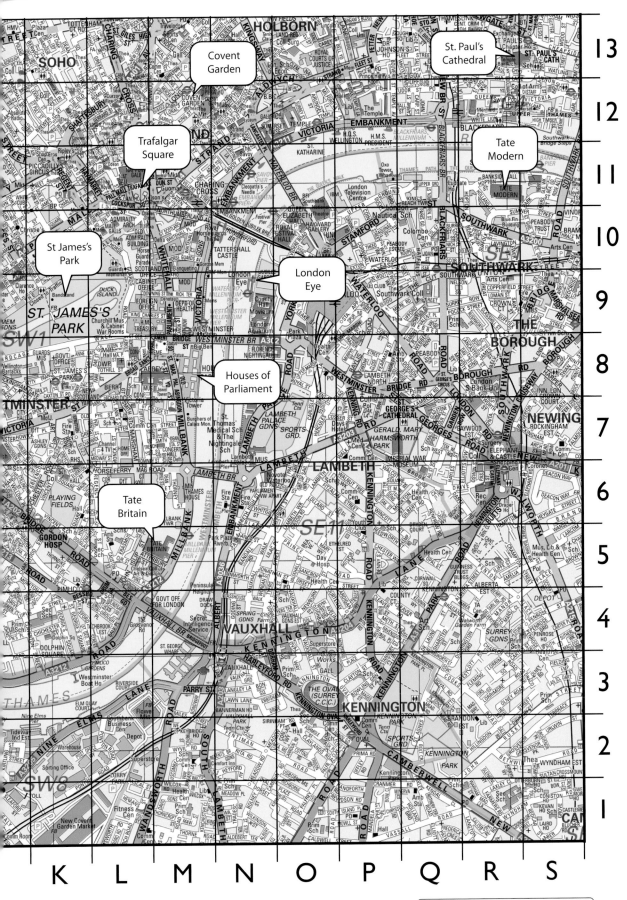

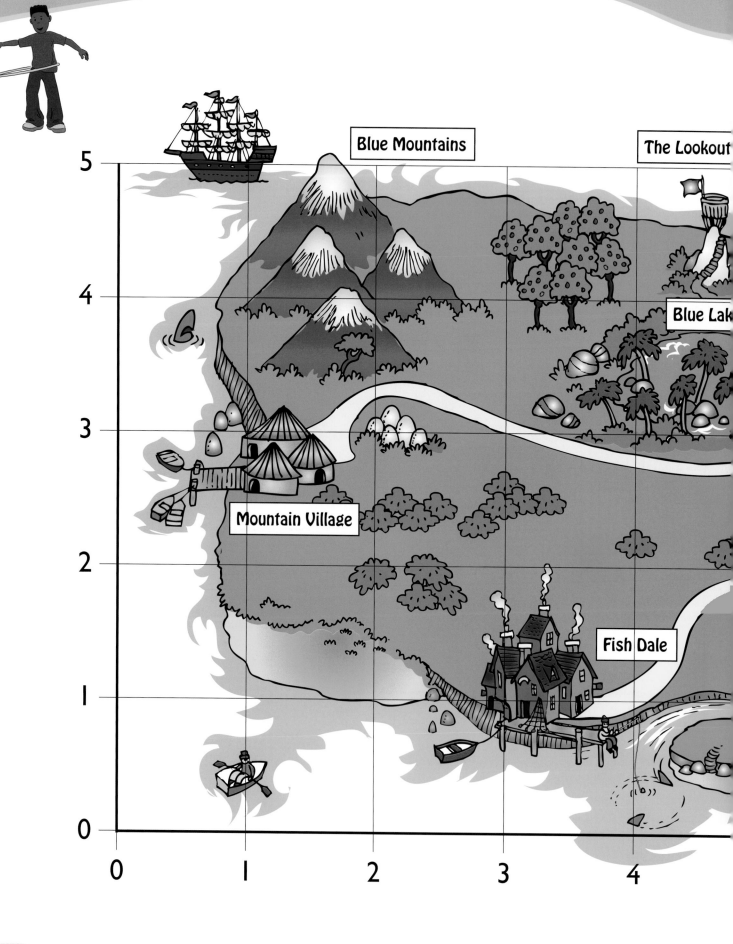

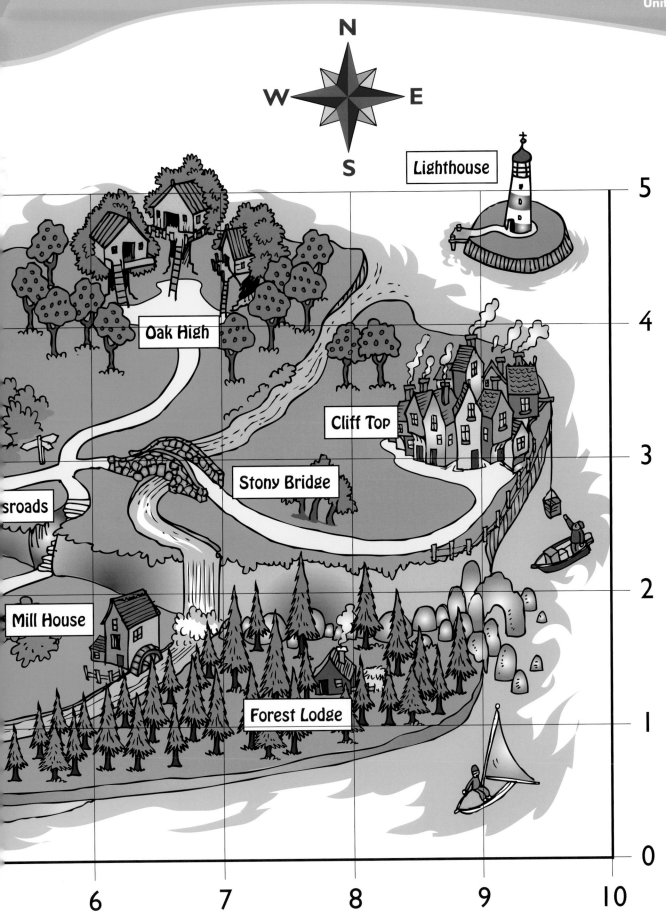

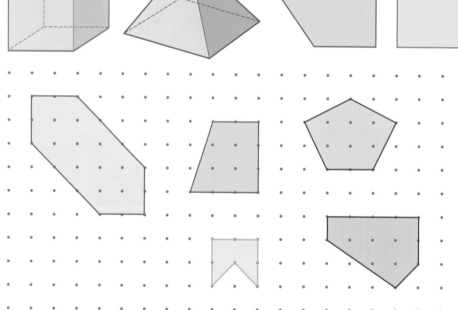

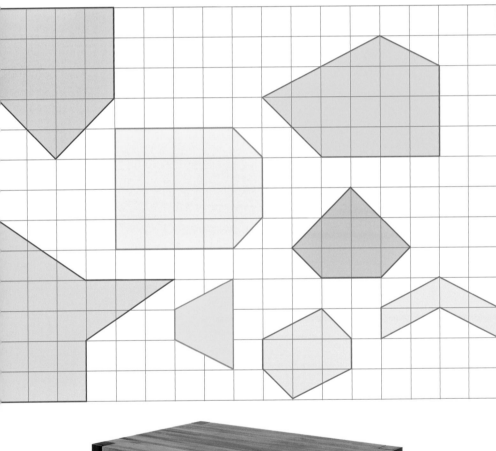

A _____

B _____

C _____

D _____

E _____

F _____

G _____

H _____

I _____

J _____

K

L

M

N

O

P

Q

R

S

T

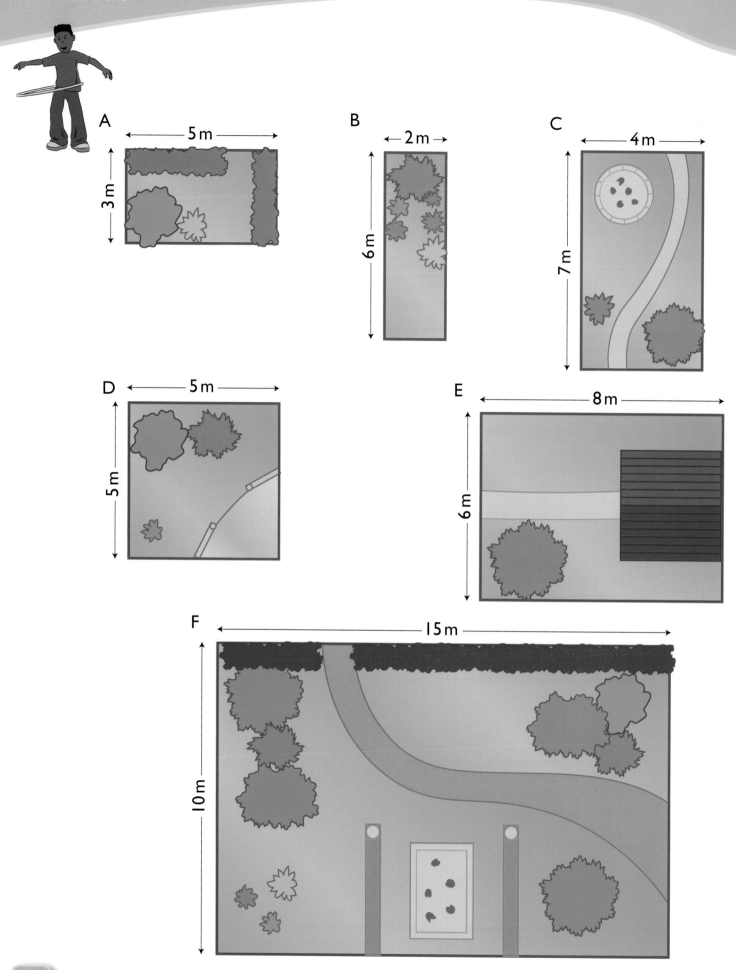

A
5 m
3 m

B
2 m
6 m

C
4 m
7 m

D
5 m
5 m

E
8 m
6 m

F
15 m
10 m

G

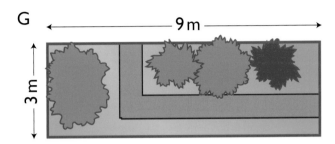

H

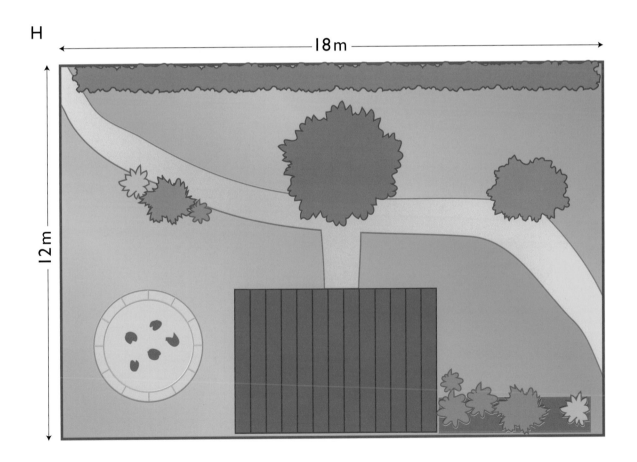

A

B

C

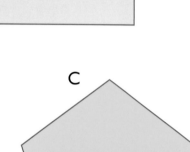

D

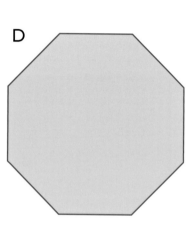

E

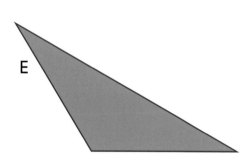

F

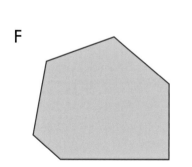

G

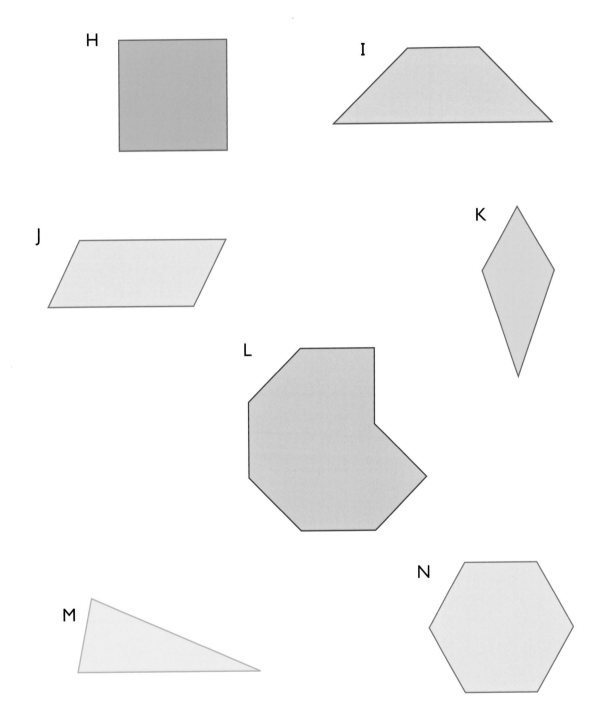

H

I

J

K

L

M

N

A

B

C

D

E

F

G

H

I

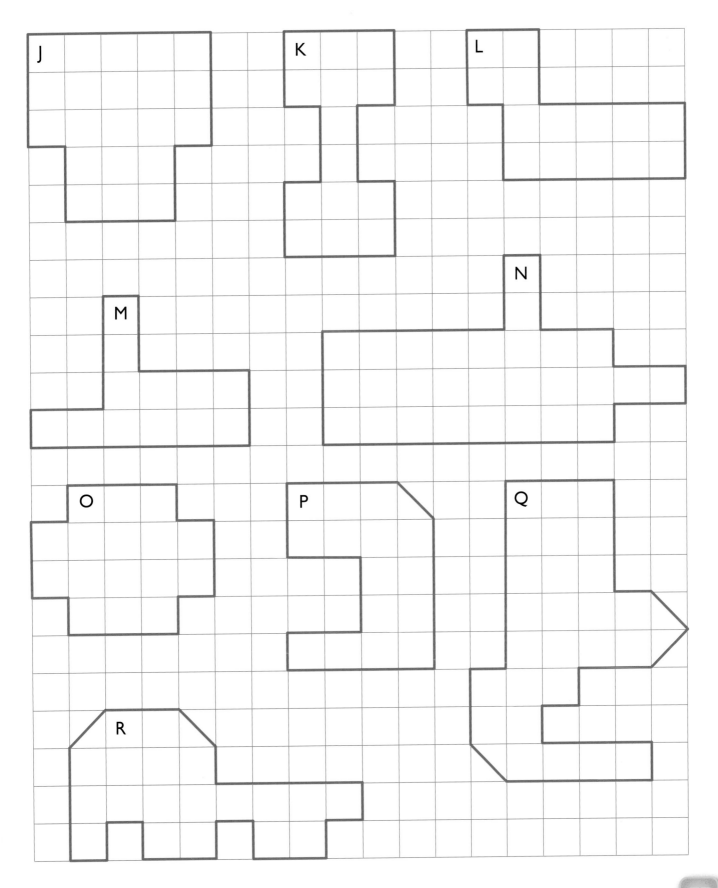

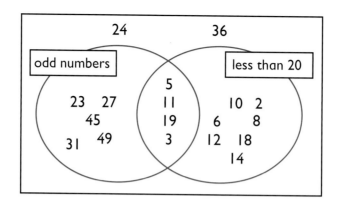

Money raised for charity

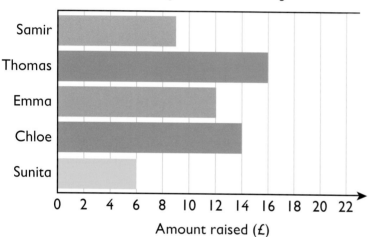

Day	Visitors to the museum
Monday	0
Tuesday	542
Wednesday	412
Thursday	654
Friday	742
Saturday	1324
Sunday	1587

	Multiple of 3	Multiple of 7
Odd	9 15 27	7 35 49
Even	6 12 18	14 28 56

How they travel to work

Transport	Tally	Frequency
train	||||	4
bus	|||| ||||	10
car	|||| ||	7
walk	|||| |||	8
bike	|||	3

Our favourite fruits

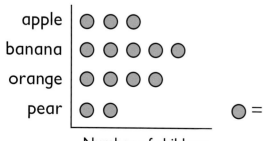

◯ = 2 children

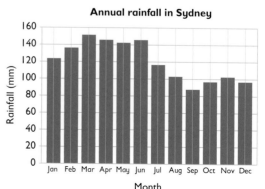

NOVEMBER						
M	**T**	**W**	**T**	**F**	**S**	**S**
				1	2	3
4	5	6	7	8	9	10
11	12	13	14	15	16	17
18	19	20	21	22	23	24
25	26	27	28	29	30	

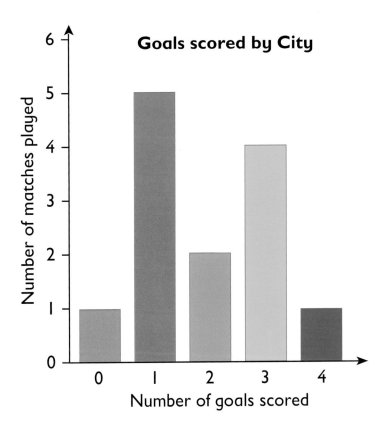

Goals scored by City

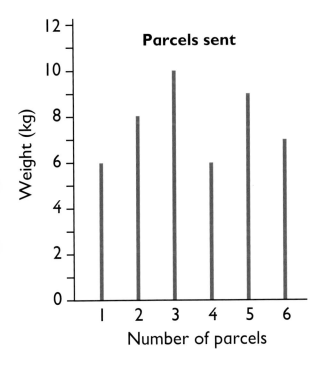

Parcels sent

Number of brothers and sisters

	Number of children
0	🧍🧍🧍🧍
1	🧍🧍🧍🧍🧍🧍🧍🧍🧍
2	🧍🧍🧍🧍🧍🧍🧍
3	🧍🧍🧍
4 or more	🧍🧍🧍🧍🧍

🧍 represents 1 child

Trains from Bomaderry to Sydney

	Bomaderry	Berry	Gerringong	Kiama	Dapto	Wollongong	Sutherland	Hurstville	Sydney
a.m.	9:31	9:41	9:50	9:59	10:28	10:52	11:48	11:58	12:16
a.m.	11:29	11:39	11:48	11:57	12:26	12:50	1:46	1:56	2:14
p.m.	1:36	1:46	1:55	2:04	2:33	2:57	3:53	4:03	4:21
p.m.	3:24	3:34	3:43	3:51	4:21	4:45	5:41	5:51	6:09
p.m.	5:00	5:10	5:20	6:00	6:30	6:59	7:50	8:00	8:15

Distance chart (km)	Birmingham	Bristol	Cardiff	Edinburgh	Glasgow
Birmingham		141·5	185	467	463
Bristol	141·5		73	601	597
Cardiff	185	73		644	640
Edinburgh	467	601	644		75
Glasgow	463	597	640	75	

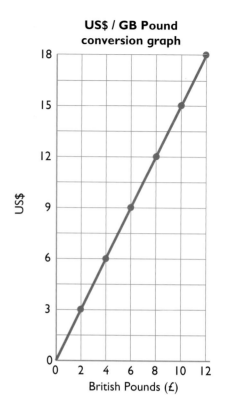

US$ / GB Pound conversion graph

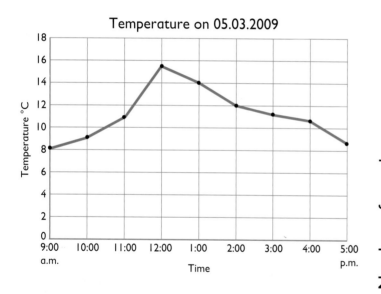

Temperature on 05.03.2009

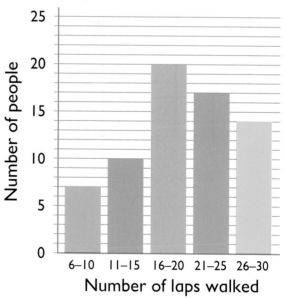

Sponsored school walk

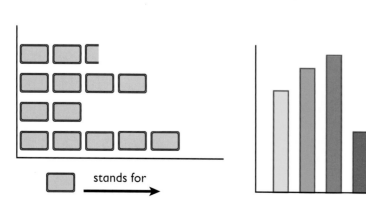

stands for

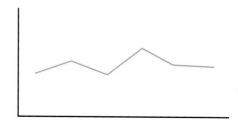